TRAIN TIME

Lisa Baehr
Illustrated with Photographs

HAMPTON-BROWN

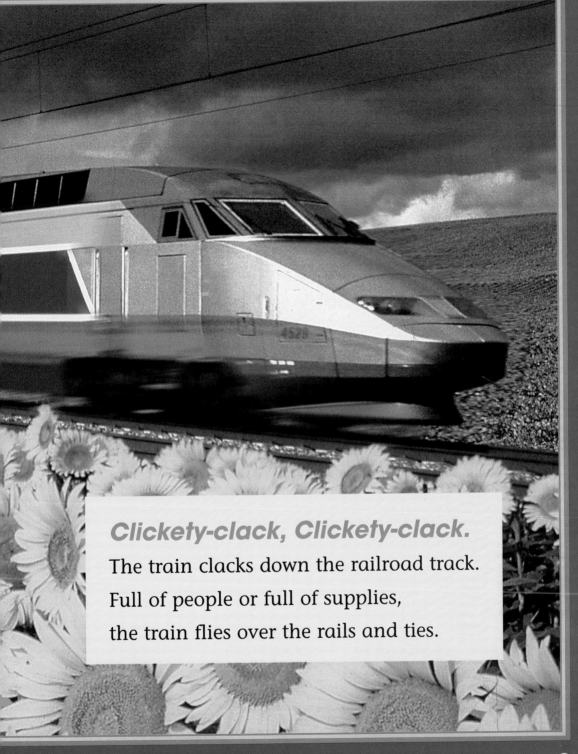

Clickety-clack, Clickety-clack.
The train clacks down the railroad track.
Full of people or full of supplies,
the train flies over the rails and ties.

Clickety-clack, Clickety-clack.
See the train go down the track.

It has been to the city today,
moving people along the way.
People get in. People get out.
The train takes people all about.

Clickety-clack, Clickety-clack.
The train clacks down the railroad track.
Full of people or full of supplies,
the train flies over the rails and ties.

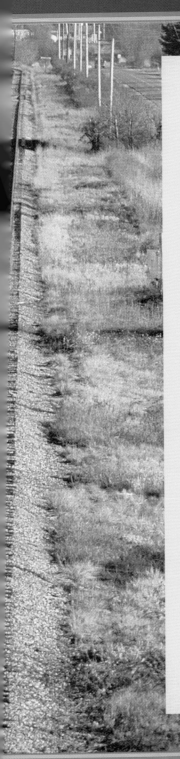

Clickety-clack, Clickety-clack.

See the train go down the track.

It has been to a forest today,
taking logs away, away.
Logs get loaded. Logs get stacked.
The train pulls out fully packed.

Clickety-clack, Clickety-clack.

The train clacks down the railroad track.
Full of people or full of supplies,
the train flies over the rails and ties.

Clickety-clack, Clickety-clack.

See the train go down the track.

It came into a town today,
bringing cars to drive away.
Cars come down. Cars come off.
No cars are left for the train's next stop.

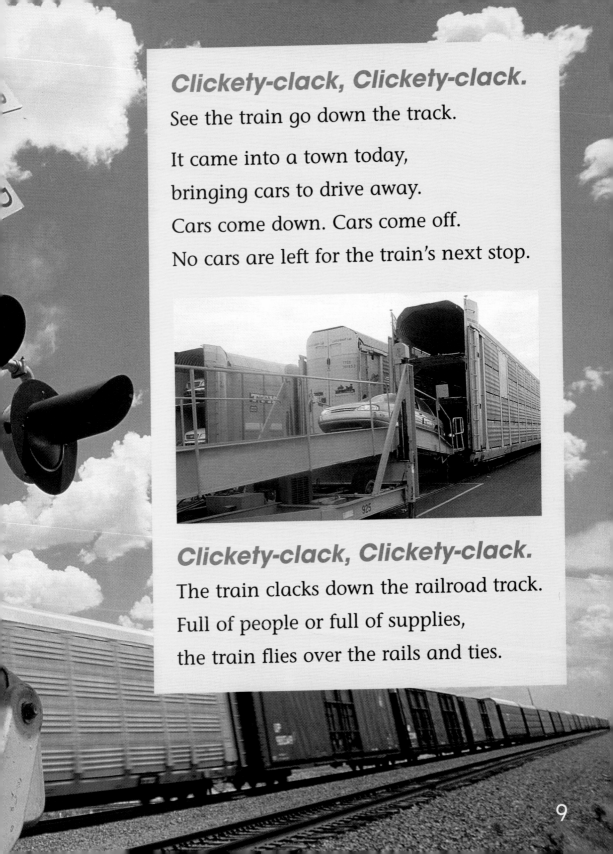

Clickety-clack, Clickety-clack.

The train clacks down the railroad track.
Full of people or full of supplies,
the train flies over the rails and ties.

Clickety-clack, Clickety-clack.

How does a train go down the track?

A locomotive has to pull
one car, two cars, three cars full.
It has to pull and pull and pull
because each car is very full.

Clickety-clack, Clickety-clack.

The train clacks down the railroad track.
Full of people or full of supplies,
the train flies over the rails and ties.

locomotive

train car

Clickety-clack, Clickety-clack.

How does a train stay on the track?

Train wheels hug those long, long rails,
working together, without fail.
Wheels and rails work as one,
fitting together—that's how it's done.

ties

rails

Clickety-clack, Clickety-clack.

The train speeds down the railroad track.
Full of people or full of supplies,
the train flies over the rails and ties.

Clickety-clack, Clickety-clack.

Where have these trains been on the track?

One has been to the city today,
moving people along the way.
Another has been to a forest today,
taking logs away, away.
Another has been to a town today,
leaving cars to drive away.
All the trains went over their tracks,
hugging the rails, down and back.

Clickety-clack, Clickety-clack.

Trains fly down the railroad track.

They pull out—they'll come back.

There they go, clickety-clack!

THINK ABOUT IT

1. Where did the trains in the story go? What did they carry?

2. Why do you think trains are good for carrying people and supplies?

3. Where would you like to go in a train? Why?

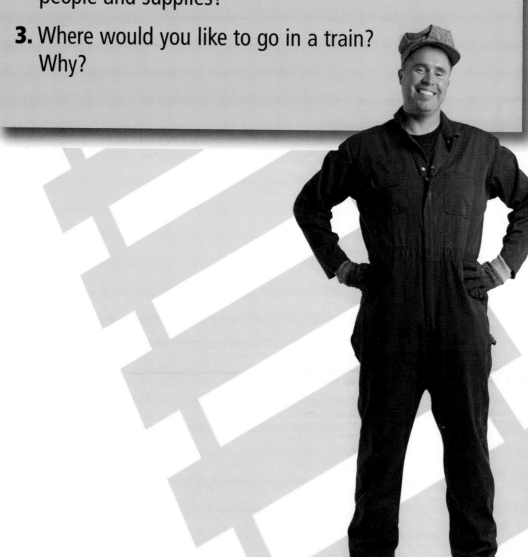